D1550689

* Smithsonian

LITTLE EXPLORER

VELOCIRAPTOR

by Janet Riehecky

CAPSTONE PRESS
a capstone imprint

Little Explorer is published by Capstone Press,
1710 Roe Crest Drive, North Mankato, Minnesota 56003
www.capstoneyoungreaders.com

Copyright © 2015 by Capstone Press, a Capstone
imprint. All rights reserved. No part of this publication
may be reproduced in whole or in part, or stored in
a retrieval system, or transmitted in any form or by
any means, electronic, mechanical, photocopying,
recording, or otherwise, without written permission
of the publisher.

The name of the Smithsonian Institution and the
sunburst logo are registered trademarks of the
Smithsonian Institution. For more information,
please visit www.si.edu.

**Library of Congress Cataloging-in-Publication
Data**
Riehecky, Janet, 1953–
Velociraptor / by Janet Riehecky.
pages cm. — (Smithsonian little explorer.
Little paleontologist.)
Includes index.
Summary: "Introduces young readers to Velociraptor,
including physical characteristics, diet, habitat, and life
cycle"— Provided by publisher.
ISBN 978-1-4914-0813-1 (library binding)
ISBN 978-1-4914-0825-4 (paperback)
ISBN 978-1-4914-0819-3 (paper over board)
ISBN 978-1-4914-0831-5 (eBook PDF)
1. Velociraptor—Juvenile literature. I. Title.
QE862.S3R54 2015
567.912—dc23
2014002085

Editorial Credits
Michelle Hasselius, editor; Heidi Thompson, designer;
Wanda Winch, media researcher; Kathy McColley,
production specialist

Our very special thanks to Mike Brett-Surman, PhD,
Museum Specialist for Fossil Dinosaurs, Reptiles,
Amphibians, and Fish at the National Museum of
Natural History, Smithsonian Institution, for his
curatorial review. Capstone would also like to
thank Kealy Wilson, Product Development Manager,
and the following at Smithsonian Enterprises:
Ellen Nanney, Licensing Manager; Brigid Ferraro,
Vice President, Education and Consumer Products;
Carol LeBlanc, Senior Vice President, Education
and Consumer Products.

Image Credits
Capstone: James Field, cover, Steve Weston, 8 (top), 22;
Corbis Stocktrek Images/Mark Stevenson, 12 (bottom);
Corel, 20 (middle), Dreamstime: Cata37, 6 (left); Jon
Hughes, 1, 5 (b), 6–7, 9 (t), 11, 14–15, 19 (b), 23 (t), 26;
Library of Congress: Prints and Photographs Division
25 (inset); Newscom: AFP/AMNH/D. Finnin, 27,
Universal Studios, 29 (t), Zuma Press/Action Images/
Paul Harding, 29 (b); Science Source: Jose Antonio
Penas, 18–19; Shutterstock: Stefania Hill, 20 (bl), BACO,
4 (br), Catmando, 8 (b), 9 (b), chiakto, 25 (top), Juancat,
10, Leonello Calvetti, 20 (tr), Linda Bucklin, 2–3, 4
(bl), Michael Rosskothen, 16, 28, 30–31, pinare, 20 (br),
reallyround, 5 (tr), Sofia Santos, 20 (tl), Steffen Foerster,
5 (tl), The_Pixel, 24–25, T4W4, 4 (top), with God, 17,
SuperStock: Stocktrek Images, 12–13, 14 (b), 21; The
Trustees of the Natural History Museum, London:
Kokoro, 23 (b)

Printed in the United States of America in Stevens Point, Wisconsin.
032014   008092WZF14

TABLE OF CONTENTS

name: Velociraptor

how to say it: veh-LAH-si-rap-tor

when it lived: Cretaceous Period, Mesozoic Era

what it ate: meat

size: 5 to 6 feet (1.5 to 1.8 meters) long
almost 3 feet (0.9 m) tall
weighed 30 to 40 pounds
(14 to 18 kilograms)

Velociraptor lived 75 million to
71 million years ago. The fierce
meat eater was smaller than many
other dinosaurs during this time.

Thanks to FOSSILS

A fossil is evidence of life from the past. Fossils of things like bones, teeth, and tracks found in the earth have taught us everything we know about dinosaurs.

A LARGE BIRD

long, stiff tail

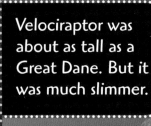

Velociraptor was about as tall as a Great Dane. But it was much slimmer.

a sickle claw on each foot

flat, long head

sharp teeth

three fingers on each hand

feathers on arms and body

"If animals like Velociraptor were alive today, our first impression would be that they were just very unusual-looking birds."
—paleontologist Mark Norell

THE RAPTOR GROUP

Velociraptor was part of a group of dinosaurs called the raptors. The raptor group had many other dinosaurs in it.

Oviraptor (OH-vih-rap-tor) was about the same size as Velociraptor. Its skeleton was found in a nest of dinosaur eggs, so scientists named it "egg thief." Later scientists discovered the eggs belonged to Oviraptor.

Deinonychus (dye-NON-ih-kus) lived in packs and hunted small and even large dinosaurs.

Deinonychus was about the size of a mountain lion.

Achillobator (a-KILL-oh-bay-tor) was bigger than Deinonychus. It grew to almost 20 feet (6 m) long and weighed 500 to 1,000 pounds (225 to 450 kg).

Utahraptor (YOU-tah-rap-tor) is the biggest raptor discovered so far. It grew to about 23 feet (7 m) long and weighed almost 1 ton (0.9 metric ton). Its sickle claw was 12 inches (30.5 centimeters) long.

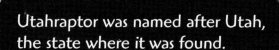

Utahraptor was named after Utah, the state where it was found.

FEATHERS

Scientists discovered quill knobs on Velociraptor's arm in 2007. Quill knobs prove the dinosaur had feathers.

Male Velociraptors may have had brightly colored feathers. Bright feathers helped attract a mate.

Female Velociraptors likely had dull feathers. Females could spread their feathers over their eggs. These feathers hid the eggs from sunlight and predators.

Velociraptor's feathers didn't help it fly. Its arms were too short and its body was too long to get off the ground. Some birds today can't fly either, such as ostriches and penguins.

STIFF TAIL

Velociraptor's tail was stiff and stuck straight out. It helped Velociraptor keep its balance when walking or running.

Dinosaurs such as Diplodocus used their tails as weapons. They swung their tails like whips. But not Velociraptor—its tail was too stiff to swing like that.

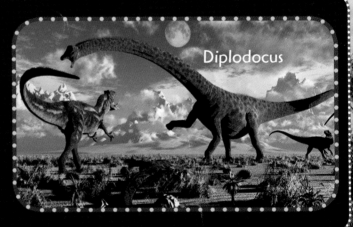

Diplodocus

When Velociraptor moved, its tail swung back and forth. The swinging tail helped the dinosaur change directions quickly when it ran. Velociraptor might have been able to do amazing twists and turns to escape predators or catch prey.

FAST RUNNER

Velociraptor's slim body and long legs may have made it a fast runner. Speed allowed Velociraptor to catch its next meal and escape hungry predators.

Many scientists believe Velociraptor ran as fast as 24 miles per hour (39 kilometers per hour). Other scientists don't agree that the dinosaur was a fast runner. They think Velociraptor's long legs helped it climb and jump.

Velociraptor's name means "swift thief."

SICKLE CLAW

Velociraptor had sharp claws on its hands and feet. The second toe of each foot had an especially large claw called a sickle claw. To keep the claw sharp, Velociraptor held it up above the ground when it walked or ran.

The sickle claw could break through skin and hold onto prey. But it wasn't strong or sharp enough to kill another dinosaur.

Birds of prey, like hawks and eagles, also have a larger claw on their second toes.

HUNTING FOOD

Velociraptor was a carnivore.
Carnivores eat meat.

This dinosaur was a good hunter. Its eyes faced
forward, which gave it great eyesight. Sneaking
up on prey was an easy task. When Velociraptor
attacked, its large sickle claw helped hold onto
prey. Its razor-sharp teeth helped kill the animal.

Velociraptors may have hunted in packs. Working together would have allowed them to attack larger prey.

Because of its size, Velociraptor probably ate small dinosaurs, lizards, and insects. It may also have eaten the eggs of other dinosaurs.

It is likely Velociraptor was also a scavenger. It would wait for a big predator to finish eating its kill. Then it could rush in to eat what was left.

VELOCIRAPTOR'S HOME

Velociraptor lived during the Cretaceous Period. It made its home in the desert areas of what is now Mongolia, China.

Velociraptor's home was hot and dry. Water and plants could be found in only a few places. Sand stretched out across the land. Sometimes giant sand dunes formed. There were also volcanoes.

Other Cretaceous Animals

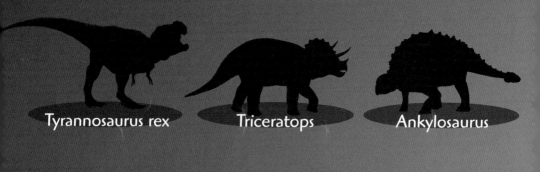

Tyrannosaurus rex   Triceratops   Ankylosaurus

Oviraptor   Protoceratops

The Cretaceous Period lasted
from 145 to 66 million years ago.

DINOSAUR ERA

TRIASSIC	JURASSIC	CRETACEOUS

250   200   145   66   present

millions of
years ago

GROWING UP

Scientists haven't found many clues about
what Velociraptor was like growing up.

Other dinosaurs in the raptor group took care of their young. That probably means Velociraptor did too.

Young Velociraptor had larger eyes and a shorter snout than adults.

Oviraptor with its eggs

23

DISCOVERY

Paleontologist Roy Chapman Andrews
discovered the first Velociraptor fossils. He
found them in the Gobi Desert of Mongolia
in the 1920s. Velociraptor bones have
only been found in Mongolia. But other
raptors have been found all over the world,
including the United States.

Andrews and his team found other dinosaurs as well, including Oviraptor. They also discovered the first dinosaur eggs.

Roy Chapman Andrews

Gobi Desert

Mongolia

FOREVER IN BATTLE

Paleontologists made an amazing fossil find in the Gobi Desert in 1971. A Velociraptor and a Protoceratops were found locked in battle. Velociraptor was holding onto the Protoceratops' head. Its sickle claw was sunk into the dinosaur's chest. Protoceratops was biting Velociraptor's right arm, which was broken. They died in the middle of the fight.

This was the first fossil discovery to show two dinosaurs fighting each other.

Protoceratops ▼

▲Velociraptor

Some scientists think the fighting dinosaurs died when a strong wind blew a sand dune on top of them.

DID YOU KNOW?

A bone in Velociraptor's eye shows it might have been nocturnal. That means it hunted at night and slept during the day. This same bone is found today in nocturnal birds and lizards.

The 1993 movie *Jurassic Park* made Velociraptor famous. But the movie's dinosaur did not look like Velociraptor. This dinosaur didn't have feathers. It was also much bigger and smarter than Velociraptor really was. The dinosaur in the movie was based on the body of a large Deinonychus.

Like birds today, Velociraptor had hollow bones. It was also probably warm-blooded.

Toronto Canada's professional basketball team is named the Toronto Raptors.

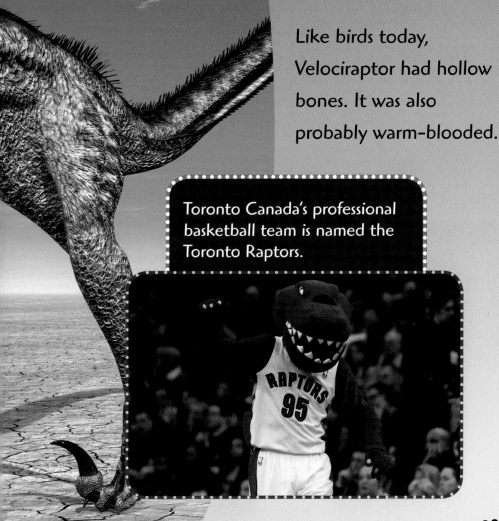

GLOSSARY

attract—to get the attention of someone or something

fossil—evidence of life from the geologic past

hollow—empty on the inside

mate—the male or female partner of a pair of animals

Mesozoic Era—the age of dinosaurs, which includes the Triassic, Jurassic, and Cretaceous periods, when the first birds, mammals, and flowers appeared

nocturnal—active at night and resting during the day

paleontologist—a scientist who studies fossils

predator—an animal that hunts other animals for food

prey—an animal hunted by another animal for food

quill knob—a round bump on a bone that holds a feather

sand dune—hills of sand, made by wind and water

scavenger—an animal that feeds on animals that are already dead

sickle—a sharp, curved edge that is shaped like the letter C

snout—the long front part of an animal's head; it includes the nose, mouth, and jaws

CRITICAL THINKING USING THE COMMON CORE

Velociraptor was smaller than many dinosaurs but still a fierce predator during the Cretaceous Period. Describe two ways Velociraptor caught its prey. (Key Ideas and Details)

Velociraptor was likely a nocturnal dinosaur. What does nocturnal mean? Name one modern animal that is nocturnal. (Craft and Structure)

Look at the image on page 26. Describe in your own words what is happening in the scene. (Integration of Knowledge and Ideas)

READ MORE

Dodson, Peter. *Velociraptor Up Close: Swift Dinosaur.* Zoom in on Dinosaurs! Berkeley Heights, N.J.: Enslow Publishers, 2011.

Kolpin, Molly. *Velociraptor: Clawed Hunter.* First Graphics. North Mankato, Minn.: Capstone Press, 2012.

Mara, Wil. *Velociraptor.* Rookie Read-About Dinosaurs. New York: Children's Press, 2012.

INTERNET SITES

FactHound offers a safe, fun way to find Internet sites related to this book. All of the sites on FactHound have been researched by our staff.

Here's all you do:

Visit *www.facthound.com*

Type in this code: 9781491408131

Super-cool stuff!

Check out projects, games and lots more at
www.capstonekids.com

INDEX